We Did It!
Our Grand Canyon Adventure

Published by Melanie Pergiel
Text Copyright © 2022 by Melanie Pergiel
Illustrations Copyright © 2022 by Madison Wilcox
Edited by Cindy Hatch
All rights reserved.

Printed in the United States

ISBN 978-0-578-92320-8

We did it!

Our Grand Canyon Adventure

By Melanie Pergiel

Illustrated by Madison Wilcox

Melanie Pergiel
10/2022

Edited by Cindy Hatch

For Luke and Jackson
And all the trekkers of the trails

Luke and Jackson lived with their mom, dad, and a black cat named Scissors near the rim of the **Grand Canyon** in Arizona. They liked to play among the pinyon and juniper trees, ride their bikes through the woods to school, build campfires, and eat marshmallows.

They liked to lie on the roof outside their bedroom
window with Dad and Scissors, looking at the stars.

Even though Luke and
Jackson lived very
close to one of the
most famous wonders
of the world, they had
never ventured over
the edge and into
the huge canyon.

One day their mom asked them if they would like to hike down a trail to the bottom of the Grand Canyon, spend the night, then hike back out.

"Sweet!" said Luke.
"Awesome!" said Jackson.
"But what if we can't do it? I am only 6!"

"You will be fine, Jackson" replied his dad.
"We will take plenty of water and snacks.
Luke is a good hiker."

On a bright sunny day, Luke and Jackson said good-bye
to Scissors and set off down the **Bright Angel Trail**
with their parents. They were heading towards the
Colorado River at the bottom of the Grand Canyon.

They carried backpacks filled with water, snacks,
bandaids, sunscreen, headlamps, and an extra pair of socks
and underwear. In order to keep their packs from being too heavy,
Mom said the boys could hike back out in their same clothes.
But she insisted they carry clean socks and underwear. She told
them that clean socks would help to prevent blisters
on their feet while hiking. Jackson wondered why Mom did not
explain why they needed clean underwear.

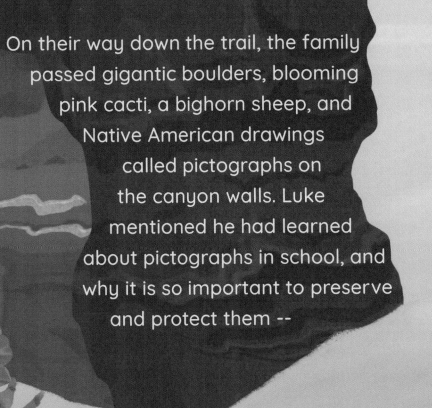

On their way down the trail, the family passed gigantic boulders, blooming pink cacti, a bighorn sheep, and Native American drawings called pictographs on the canyon walls. Luke mentioned he had learned about pictographs in school, and why it is so important to preserve and protect them --

because they are part of history.

Indian Gardens, a shady oasis 4 miles down the trail, offered a nice place to rest and eat their picnic lunch.

They also met hikers there from all
over the world.

They cooled their feet in the creek and learned about
the colorful rock layers of the canyon.

INDIAN
GARDEN

While hiking further DOWN the trail, Luke and Jackson met people hiking UP. Jackson noticed that their faces were red and their heads were hanging low. They did not talk much, like the hikers did back at Indian Gardens. Jackson wondered why they looked so tired.

Soon they met a mule train carrying supplies.

Luke and Jackson stood quietly off to the side of the trail to give them room to pass.

They learned that mules are larger and stronger than most horses. They are more sure-footed on the steep winding trail. Luke said he was glad he was hiking instead of riding a big mule.

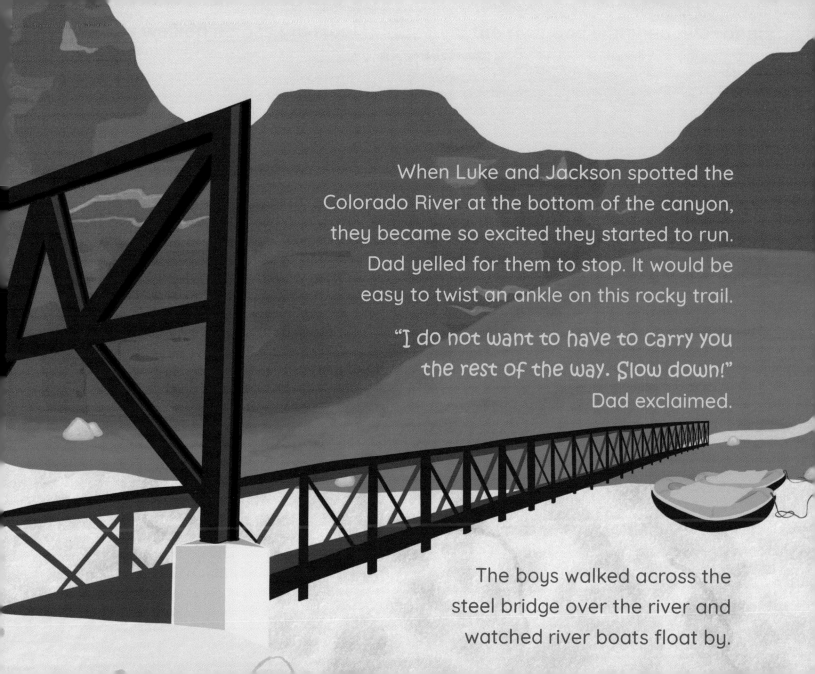

When Luke and Jackson spotted the
Colorado River at the bottom of the canyon,
they became so excited they started to run.
Dad yelled for them to stop. It would be
easy to twist an ankle on this rocky trail.

"I do not want to have to carry you
the rest of the way. Slow down!"
Dad exclaimed.

The boys walked across the
steel bridge over the river and
watched river boats float by.

The campground and cabins at **Phantom Ranch** were a welcome sight after the long hike down.

The breeze through the green cottonwood trees beside **Bright Angel Creek** felt nice.

After dark, a National Park Service volunteer showed Luke and Jackson how to find scorpions with a black light. There were so many! Under the light, the scorpions had a fluorescent green glow, but when the light was off, they disappeared. They blended in with the grass and rocks. The volunteer taught Luke and Jackson not to be afraid of them. Just be cautious. Don't pick them up or step on them with your bare feet.

They will sting!

Luke and Jackson did not want to step on a scorpion with their bare feet, so they decided they would keep their shoes on until they got into their sleeping bags.

Later that night, Luke and Jackson studied the many stars and listened to cool stories before falling asleep at the bottom of one of the most beautiful canyons in the world.

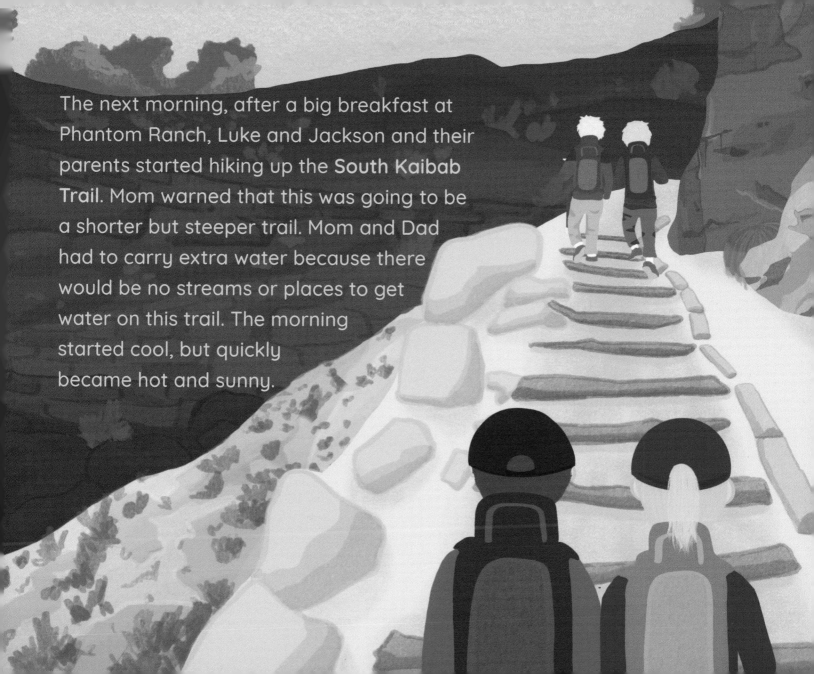

The next morning, after a big breakfast at Phantom Ranch, Luke and Jackson and their parents started hiking up the **South Kaibab Trail**. Mom warned that this was going to be a shorter but steeper trail. Mom and Dad had to carry extra water because there would be no streams or places to get water on this trail. The morning started cool, but quickly became hot and sunny.

After hiking for a while, Jackson exclaimed, "I can't do it!"
He then lay down in the middle of the trail. Mom quickly
shoved some granola bar and cheese into his mouth,
followed by some water.

Jackson suddenly jumped up and ran up the trail. After a while, he stopped and lay down again. "I can't do it!" he exclaimed. Mom shoved some chocolate and nuts into his mouth. Again, Jackson suddenly jumped up and started running up the trail. He continued to repeat these actions for the rest of the hike.

While making frequent snack stops with Jackson, Mom and Dad lost sight of Luke. They realized no one had seen him for a while. Where did he go? Mom and Dad became worried. There was no way to go but up, so they kept hiking. Mom asked several hikers coming down the trail if they had seen a skinny boy with crazy blonde hair. They said, "Yes!" Several people had met him hiking up while they were hiking down. "He had his head down and a red face."

Mom and Dad continued to hike up,
still feeding Jackson along the way.

They rounded a corner and saw a
little boy sitting on a boulder.
It was Luke!
"What took y'all so long?" he grinned.

"We were worried about you.
You should never hike alone
without telling someone,
and never leave your
hiking buddy,"
Dad taught him.

Luke and Jackson made it to the top of the trail on the rim of the Grand Canyon.

They were so excited and happy, "We did it!"
They were not even tired anymore.
But Mom and Dad were.